SWING TRADING

Start Making Profits Investing In Financial Markets With Options, Futures, & Stocks. To Create An Additional Income Stream And Improve Your Life

MARK KRATTER

© **Copyright 2021 - All rights reserved.**

The content contained within this book may not be reproduced, duplicated or transmitted without direct written permission from the author or the publisher.

Under no circumstances will any blame or legal responsibility be held against the publisher, or author, for any damages, reparation, or monetary loss due to the information contained within this book. Either directly or indirectly.

Legal Notice:

This book is copyright protected. This book is only for personal use. You cannot amend, distribute, sell, use, quote or paraphrase any part, or the content within this book, without the consent of the author or publisher.

Disclaimer Notice:

Please note the information contained within this document is for educational and entertainment purposes only. All effort has been executed to present accurate, up to date, and reliable, complete information. No warranties of any kind are declared or implied. Readers acknowledge that the author is not engaging in the rendering of legal, financial, medical or professional advice. The content within this book has been derived from various sources. Please consult a licensed professional before attempting any techniques outlined in this book.

By reading this document, the reader agrees that under no circumstances is the author responsible for any losses, direct or indirect, which are incurred as a result of the use of information contained within this document, including, but not limited to, errors, omissions, or inaccuracies.

Table of Contents

Introduction 7
Chapter 1 - About Swing Trading 16
Chapter 2 - Swing vs. Day vs. Position Trading 23
Chapter 3 - How to Start Trading 32
Chapter 4 - Long vs. Short 41
Chapter 5 - The Art of Selling Short 45
Chapter 6 - Bull vs. Bear Market 51
Chapter 7 - Account, Tools and Platforms 55
Chapter 8 - Options and Forex Swing Trading 65
Chapter 9 - Risk Management for Swing Trading 71
Chapter 10 - Technical Issues 79
Conclusion 85

Introduction

What Most People Do

When it comes to the stock market and traders, most individuals are looking for the high-volume trades, with fluctuating prices. They get in, make a profit, and get out to find the next big profit.

Final Thoughts

The shares are first released from a company to gain investment funds. The shares are then traded as a way to garner dividends and profit from the up and downtrends in the market. The market also allows you to invest in various exchanges around the world, as long as your broker provides access. Most people trade in their country's stock market or the largest in their region like the Japan Stock Exchange, London Stock Exchange, and NYSE.

Swing trading is popular amongst many investors. It can be applied to a wide array of financial instruments including currencies, futures, stocks, and options. Each of these instruments has its own advantages and disadvantages. It is the only style that utilizes both long-term as well as day trading strategies.

Swing trading is often used by new as well as experienced traders. It carries several benefits that are not easy to ignore. It basically entails monitoring price movements or 'swings' then seeking to make a profit from these swings. To do this, you must enter and exit positions at the right time. Swing trading is always less concerned about the fundamental aspects of financial instruments since it is a relatively short-term form of trading.

Since swing trading entails making a profit, it is important to choose the right financial instruments to trade. Essentially, there are numerous factors you need to establish before settling on a particular instrument to swing trade. Some of these factors include:

Liquidity of the instrument. Liquidity is the ease with which traders sell and purchase certain financial instruments on the swing market. As a swing trader, you should focus on instruments that feature high liquidity since these are easy to buy and sell.

Compatibility with rule-based systems. Most swing traders always use systems that are rule-based to carry out their trades. Such systems allow traders to create more reliable trading signals. As you select a financial instrument, ensure that you can use it on such platforms.

The volatility of the instrument. Volatility is the rate at which the cost or value of particular security changes. This can either be a rise or decline in the price. Highly volatile securities are often easier to sell than those with low volatility. However, these are also associated with multiple risk levels. Most long-term investors often avoid stocks that bear large price swings. On the other hand, for swing and day traders, such a swing is what causes profits to be realized. You can benefit from upward and downward price swings alike.

Alignment to market trends. The swing market will always assume a bearish or bullish state. It is important to identify financial securities that are capable of moving with these trends. Trading software can assist you in filtering the kind of stocks available for trading to only those that are aligned with the current market trend.

Transaction costs. Different financial instruments feature different trading costs. If you have limited capital, you will need to choose an instrument that requires less cash to trade. Several financial instruments always require very little capital to trade. These include brokerage fees and commissions.

Information availability. Some financial instruments are popular than others. The availability of information is necessary in case you need to learn about a strategy or skill required to trade a particular stock. For example, if you do not have access to financial news updates relating to a certain financial instrument, it becomes difficult for you to estimate when the prices may change. Therefore, as you choose a financial instrument, make sure that its information is freely accessible.

Subject to technical analysis. Some financial instruments work best with technical analysis while others do not. As you make your choice, ensure that the instrument you select is easy to analyze using technical indicators and patterns. Most swing traders use technical indicators because they are simple, systematic, and easy to use. When applied correctly, technical analysis generates the right signals that you can use to enter and exit the swing market.

Besides the few points above, you also need to consider the level of risk associated with the instrument as well as the current market conditions where the instrument can be traded. Because swing trading favors a number of securities, it is easy for you to diversify your investments in a manner that reduces the risks associated with the traded.

Swing Trading Stocks

Stocks are financial securities that indicate ownership of a certain company and its assets. Trading in stocks can get a bit confusing if you do not understand the various types available on the market today. If you are a novice swing trader, mastering this can take you a lot of time. However, for professional stock traders is no big deal. To trade in stocks, you must specify the level of risk you are ready to tolerate and the amount of time you would like to leave positions open.

There are generally two major types of stocks—preferred stocks and common stocks. Commons stocks are those that are freely available to the public for trading. Most of the stocks available on the market today are of this form. They give you ownership of the company and part of the profits. These are often associated with high profits than other categories of financial instruments.

Preferred stocks, on the other hand, give you some level of right over a company but not the right to vote. The guidelines associated with preferred stocks always vary from one company to another. In case the company decides to go liquid, owners of preferred stocks are often paid off their share costs before those holding common stocks receive their payment.

Stocks can also be customized depending on certain classes. For instance, there are blue-chip stocks which represent shares from large companies that keep experiencing tremendous growth. Traders always prefer such stocks over other types because the returns are guaranteed. There are also speculative stocks that represent shares from organizations with a very undefined financial history. Such stocks feature high levels of risk since their stability is questionable. Nevertheless, the stocks always bear high-profit capabilities and some traders ignore the risk associated with them.

With growth stocks, the company listing them always has the potential for receiving high returns in form of earnings. Such companies reinvest their earnings back into the business for it to grow. They also pay some dividends to stock owners depending on the number of shares invested. Value stocks are often undervalued but carry great profit potential. Investors always purchase such stocks with the hope that the price will eventually be revised to a fair one in the future. Lastly, penny stocks feature very low prices, low volatility, and high risk. These are often avoided by most people because they rarely generate any income.

When trading stocks, you should look for those that have high-profit potential and high-risk tolerance. When choosing the right stocks to trade in, be sure to check their volume levels. Most swing traders always choose stocks that are highly liquid. This is because it is easier to close positions associated with high volume stocks faster. Since swing trading requires that you close positions soon enough to realize a profit, it is essential that you have liquidity of stock in mind when seeking the right one for the trade. Such stocks also feature lower bid-ask spreads that are favorable for swing trading.

Another aspect you need to have in mind when trading in stocks is the availability of the stock with market makers. These are individuals who hold certain stocks for some time to increase their liquidity and balance the market. Most of them are always paid a small amount for holding the shares. As a swing trader, your focus should be getting such stocks since this will ensure that you are dealing with an instrument that will remain on demand during the entire trading period.

When swing trading a particular stock, check how it correlates with market indices and other categories of stocks. This is because some stocks may seem to have the right trading features, but these end up swinging against the market direction. If you trade in these stocks, you will end up losing a good percentage of your capital. You need to focus on stocks that are volatile enough to cause a price swing. Swing trading becomes irrelevant when you apply the style on stocks whose prices are not moving.

As you get the right stock for swing trading, you want to find out if there are any upcoming activities and events that may affect the stock prices significantly. Such events may be things like the release of a new product, or an upcoming earning for the company. Here are a few quick tips that you can use to swing trading stocks:

- Use both short-term and long-term charts as well as time frames.
- Enter the market as soon as price trends start and not at the end of it.
- Use more than one indicator to analyze the market.
- Align your swings with the market direction.
- Have a trading plan before you start swing trading.
- Master all the aspects of swing trading.
- Check out for daily news on the underlying company and industry before entering positions. Also, be mindful of general market news such as economic and political news as these can impact stock prices drastically.

- Go long when the market is strong, and short when the market is weak.
- Monitor trends in the market prices and trade in relation to the trend.

Chapter 1 - About Swing Trading

Swing trading is one of the ways in which you can earn a living. The surest way of making it big is mastering your skill such as computer programming for information technologists. The more skilled you are in trading, the more your compensation. The advantage of mastering a skill is that you will be safe and sure regarding income.

Swing trading is one of the best ways you can use to make a lot of money. It provides you with the prospect of generating money based on the quality of the trades you open. The more experienced you are at trading, the higher your potential of making huge gains. Forex markets move in different patterns that can be categorized into two groups:

- Consolidating.

- Trending.

A market is said to be trending when the price puts in greater lows and highs in an uptrend and does the opposite for a downward movement. The thrust in the major direction is known as an impulse motion, and recovery in price against the direction of the impulse is called a price correction. The word "move" can be substituted by the word "swing." The diagram below shows a price movement or swing in a trending market.

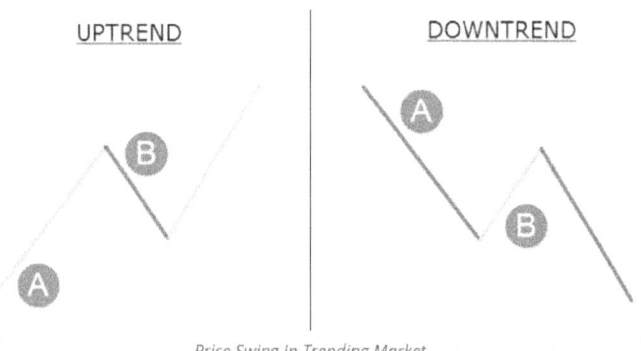

Price Swing In Trending Market

Swing trading is the practice of making profits from a short-term movement of prices of securities. In swing trading, trades are left open for a few days to a few weeks. Sometimes they can be left open for a maximum of one or two months. Swing traders can be institutions such as hedge funds or individuals. They rarely invest 100% in the market at any time, but they wait for low-risk trading opportunities in the market and ensure they make a lot of money from the opportunity. When the market is riding high, they open many buy positions. When the market is weak, they open sell positions or short more often than they buy. When the market is calm (prices not changing much), they do not open any trades.

Advantages of Swing Trading

- It has many merits over other trading styles such as day trading.

- It requires just a few minutes every day to manage your open trades, unlike day trading.
- It offers larger targets and plenty of time to open trades.

You tend to have the option of a larger stop loss placement, meaning that swing trades are less sensitive to small changes in price (whipsaw) that happens most of the time we have news announcements or during the market day.

In many instances, swing traders are in between trend traders and day traders. Day traders never hold their stocks for longer than a day. Day trading usually lasts a few hours or a few minutes. A trend trader is trained to look into the key stock trends over a long period and can hold onto stocks for months or weeks.

Long-term trading leads to good profits most of the time. Swing traders hold onto shares or stocks for more extended periods than day traders, but less time compared to trend traders. They usually open trades based on the share's monthly or intra-weekly predictions, whether they are inaccurate or not.

The majority of swing traders work best in constant markets that in those who do not move. Constant markets happen when the price of indexes, stocks, or other financial instruments rises for some days and reduces in value for the next couple of days only to rise and fall continuously. It can take several months without any change in major indexes and stocks, but an experienced swing trader learns how to make considerable profits from short-term changes in prices.

The sure-fire way of making profits for a trader working on long-term trends or a swing trader is to understand the type of market being experienced at all times. Trend trading worked best during the Bull Run in the market that happened towards the end of the 1990s. Swing trading produced the best results between the years 2000 and 2001.

The Starting Point

Many people are aware of the fact that historical data shows a market that is right for swing traders. The majority of experienced swing traders have liquid shares that tend to trade under and over a specific value. This can be explained clearly using the Exponential Moving Average graph or chart.

A renowned writer called Dr. Alexander Elder explains his understanding of share's fall and rise behavior around the baseline and shows the swing trader's aims of buying and selling. After the swing traders figure out how to use the Exponential Moving Average to determine the baseline on the share's graph, they can follow the baseline when stocks start falling and rising.

Swing trading differs from buy-and-hold investing or day trading. Day traders and other types of investors have a different trading approach. They also trade at different frequencies and pay attention to different sources of information. It is mandatory for you to understand these differences so you can focus on aspects that are essential to short-term investors.

In brief, swing trading is a perfect method of trading shares and stocks for numerous people because it provides an ideal medium between day trading and trend trading.

Volatility in Swing Trading

The term volatility in forex trading refers to the degree of risk or uncertainty that occurs with the size of changes in the exchange rate. High volatility indicates that the price of anyone's currency has changed drastically over a short timeframe. A higher volatility rate indicates that the exchange rate can be spread out exponentially over a huge range of values. On the other hand, lower volatility indicates that the rate of exchange does not change too drastically over a short period.

Summarily, a high volatility rate indicates that the trading of the affected currency pair is risky while a low volatility rate indicates less risk. In most cases, traders use the term volatility to refer to the change in the value of a pair in terms of standard deviation. Volatility is used to quantify the risk of a currency pair over some time. Generally, volatility is expressed in terms of years, and it can be in the form of a percentage, fraction, or absolute number. In other words, volatility indicates the degree of unpredictable changes in a particular currency pair over time; it represents the extent of risk that a trader is facing while trading in a particular pair.

Chapter 2 - Swing vs. Day vs. Position Trading

Swing Trading vs. Day Trading

As you know, day trading is the shorter alternative to swing trading. When people get involved in this, they are trading over a few hours, whereas people involved in swing trading are trading over a few days or weeks.

Day trading tends to be a highly volatile short-term position that can lead to massive losses if one is not careful. Unless you have the time and energy to invest in making multiple trades every day, it is challenging to become successful as a day trader. You need to be able and willing to check in on your trades several times per day to manage and exit trades all day long with this short-term strategy. If you fail to check-in or manage your positions properly, you could find yourself engaging in serious losses on a consistent basis.

While there are many risk management strategies day traders can use to minimize their exposure to the volatility of the market, it is still a highly time-consuming trading method. You need to be prepared to check in on the market every morning to identify the best trading positions and conduct technical analysis on several positions so that you can enter your trades. This means that every morning you need to be ready to identify, completely plan out, and enter several trades. This is a time-consuming task which can lead you to spending hours preparing for the market to open, only to have to spend more hours throughout the day monitoring and managing your positions.

For those who have plenty of time to trade day, trading can certainly lead to massive profits and consistent cash-out opportunities, but only if you have the time. For those who are not interested in being involved in such a demanding and stressful investment style, swing trading is a much better alternative. With swing trading, you are still capitalizing on fairly frequent market shifts, but you are not exposed to the constant stress of opening and closing positions every single day.

Yes, you will need to check in daily, enter new positions daily, and exit positions daily. This is how you manage your positions and ensure that they are all performing and profiting properly. However, because you are not in need of both entering and exiting every single trade every single day, the pace of this trading style is a little more relaxed.

Swing Trading vs. Position Trading

Position trading is the long-term trade alternative to swing trading, and it can be a highly profitable trading style. In fact, many experienced traders purposefully enter a few positional trades in addition to their swing trades as an opportunity to increase their overall profitability.

Positional trading is known for producing incredibly high profits for those who are involved in this trading strategy. Because you are withstanding the market for so long, you are able to gain access to inflation, which often results in huge profits by the time you are truly ready to exit your trade position.

With that being said, positional tradition is long-term and does require you to remain invested in a trade deal for anywhere from several weeks or months up to several years. One of the most noteworthy positional trading story themes comes from those who invested in Apple stocks back in the 1990s. People who invested in one hundred shares of Apple stocks at $78.25 in 1995 were able to cash out on those stocks for $11,244.08 in 2015. While this was a 20-year position, it earned the stockholders a profit of $11,165.83 over those 20 years. In some cases, if you can hold onto a position for the long haul, you can earn massive profits from that position, so long as it experiences consistent growth over the years.

Still, positional trading does require a long-term commitment, so it is not a position you want to enter into if you are going to need access to your profits sooner rather than later. If you plan on cashing out consistently so that you can travel, replace your income and work from home, or send your kids to grad school, you are going to want to favor something more consistent and predictable like swing trading. Even though swing trading will result in losses, each time you cash out, you have a guaranteed amount to apply toward whatever financial goals you are currently in the process of achieving.

Why Choose Swing Trading?

Hopefully, the concept of swing trading itself is starting to feel a lot clearer to you. If not, don't worry; the entire strategy will start to make a lot more sense as you begin to read about practical applications of swing trading and what exact patterns you are looking for, as well as what exact strategies you will execute trades with. In the meantime, before we dig really deep into how swing trading truly works and how you can earn profits from this strategy, let us talk about an important topic: why swing trading?

With three different fundamental trade strategies available for use, why should you choose swing trading over day trading or positional trading? Asking this question and discovering the answer is an important part of your conducting research to prepare yourself to become a trader.

As a trader, you should always be asking as many questions as possible, because questions lead to answers and answers lead to more information and education on the topic. The more that you can educate yourself on what you are doing, why you are doing it, and how you should do it, the better of a trader you are going to become.

Even the most experienced traders in the industry are still asking questions on a continual basis so that they can grow to understand their practice even more, which affords them a larger ability to scale their skills. The more skilled they become, the more they are likely to earn profits while also avoiding massive losses, which results in them becoming an even more successful trader.

All that aside, there are some very real reasons for why you should pick swing trading over any other trading strategy. These reasons will help clarify the benefits and drawbacks of this strategy, as well as how it compares against other trading strategies so that it becomes increasingly clearer as to why swing trading is one of the most popular trading strategies to date.

Benefits of Swing Trading

Some of the benefits of swing trading have already been covered here, including the fact that it is a medium-term trading strategy that allows you to maximize profitability while also being able to cash out on those profits on a more frequent basis. In addition to this, swing trading hedges you against the intense volatility that is associated with shorter positions, as well as the unpredictability of longer positions. As a result, you can protect yourself from increased risk exposure while also improving your profitability.

Swing trading also increases the number of trades that you can enter and profit from because you are not holding positions too long. Using this strategy, you can increase your profits by frequently getting into the most promising positions, and then exiting them when they are no longer as strong. Rather than attempting to wait for the market out, you can simply move into the next strongest position and profit from that, too. Therefore, you are able to profit off of the maximum profitable moments of the market and leave the rest behind.

Another benefit of swing trading you should consider is that, due to the sheer popularity of this strategy, there is a lot of education and resources available for individuals who are swing trading. As a new swing trader, having access to large amounts of information around the strategy you are going to be executing means that any questions you might have will likely already be answered in some of those resources. This reduces the mysterious element around the strategy and makes it far more tangible and accessible, which will earn you bigger profits in the long run.

Drawbacks of Swing Trading

Anytime you trade, no matter what type of trade you are engaging in, you are at risk of losing money. Even if you are absolutely confident that everything is going to go according to plan, things can change in a heartbeat and lead to you finding yourself reigning in the losses, rather than the gains. This disadvantage is not exclusive to swing trading, but it is certainly worth mentioning and considering whenever you are planning on getting into trading. I do not say this to scare you or caution you against trading, instead; I say it because the more realistic you are about the risks involved with trading, the more likely you are to hedge yourself against them and reduce your likelihood of incurring losses.

Another disadvantage of swing trading is you cannot guarantee that patterns are going to lead to what you expect, meaning that you might trade on a certain pattern three times and win, and then the fourth time you lose. The market is not predictable, nor do patterns guarantee what is to follow, instead they simply indicate what is likely to happen. There is plenty that you can do to validate patterns and testing them to ensure your likelihood of earning profits from your trades, but there are no ways to guarantee that everything will go as planned.

A big drawback of swing trading that many people are unaware of is the intense stress that it can expose your mind to. As a swing trader, you are more likely to experience massive levels of stress due to the constant fluctuations in prices. Because you are attempting to trade on the middle-term position, it can be extremely stressful to see prices fluctuating or even starting to move in directions you did not plan for. Trying to navigate the market when you are stressed can be challenging, which is why trader psychology and mindset tools are so powerful for traders.

Chapter 3 - How to Start Trading

Swing trading is viewed in some quarters as a form of fundamental trading where positions remain in place for more than a single day. Fundamentalists are traders whose approach, trading plan, and strategy are derived from fundamental analysis rather than technical analysis.

The reason why fundamental analysts are also swing traders is that any changes in the fundamentals of an organization take weeks to manifest and affect prices for a decent price movement. While the gains may be small, they do add up to considerable amounts over time.

In a real sense, swing trading actually lies between day trading and trend trading. Day trading never goes beyond a single trading day and ranges from a few seconds to a couple of hours. Day traders are generally wary of overnight market activity which may negatively influence their positions. As such, they prefer to exit all positions before close of the trading day.

A trend trader is a trader that takes the effort of examining fundamental trends of a given security for the long term. A swing trader lies somewhere between these two. Swing traders hold stock for a certain period and then trade it in the hope of benefiting from its oscillations in the days or weeks it was held.

To be successful, a trader needs to be able to identify the ideal stocks to trade-in. some of the best stocks for swing trading are these big-cap stocks. These stocks also should be among the most highly traded stocks at the markets. Such stocks often oscillate between clearly defined extremes on both extremes. A swing trader, after identifying the most ideal stocks, will enter a trade then ride the wave for as long as it is profitable before exiting just before a downward trend begins.

Swing traders thrive in different market conditions. In fact, they perform well in bearish markets and thrive in bullish markets. Momentum often carries stocks for lengthy periods but in a single direction. This is viewed by some experts as proof that the most ideal strategy is to focus on long-term direction trends.

The most ideal situation for a swing trader is a situation where markets have little movement. This contrasts with day trading where traders benefit from volatile markets. It is possible for a stock to go months or weeks without any significant movement. Short-term market movements then become extremely attractive to swing traders.

Apart from identifying the right stock to deal with, success for swing traders calls for a proper determination of the right and most appropriate market conditions. Fortunately, some tools are readily available to help make these determinations. For instance, we can use EPA or the exponential moving average.

Getting Started with Swing Trading

Swing traders rely on technical indicators to make crucial decisions regarding their trading activities. For instance, the momentum indicator RSI or relative strength indicator is an excellent gauge. It informs a trader when movements at the market are overdone on both the downside and upside. It also advises on when the corrections are ready in either direction.

As a trader, you really need to understand the entire trading process. The first step is to know where to begin. If you have a preferred trading style, then this is great because all you need to do is to make a few adjustments. It is advisable to use simple strategies, as complex ones sometimes become overwhelming and may even confuse you.

Apart from technical indicators such as the RSI, swing traders make use of strategies. There is a need for careful consideration when it comes to the asset that is selected for trading. The most commonly traded securities are stocks. Others include currencies, indices, and even options. Trading options is considered favorable as they are known to have limited risks on the downside.

How to Identify Stocks for Swing Trading?

One of the most crucial things that you can do in order to be a successful swing trader is identifying ideal stocks or other financial instruments to trade. The first step in identifying ideal stocks is to identify obvious catalysts. A catalyst is an event that can cause the stock price to increase exponentially within a short period.

Think about events such as economic data points, regulatory announcements, earnings reports, and other scheduled events that can impact the world of finance. Most of these events are predictable and known way ahead of time. Due to this predictability, you can know when to keep track of events, get ready, and eventually get into the market. Most swing traders are able to time these events perfectly and proceed to benefit from stock price movements.

In the United States, for instance, traders already knew that on the first Tuesday of each month, the auto industry will release their sales figures. The strength of the sales will help determine whether the stocks will trend upwards or downwards. Major auto companies in the US include Ford Motor Company, General Motors, and Fiat Chrysler among others.

Another thing you have to be on the lookout for is volatility. Volatility is your friend as a swing trader. You should be wary of long upward or downward trends as they provide no clear exit or entry points. However, some volatility will come in handy. When this is present, then you will clearly see the best spots to place a stop-loss, take profit, as well as entry and trade exit points.

Steps to Finding Best Stocks to Trade

Swing trading can be challenging before you get used to it. Most of the time, you will be working with different tools trying to make the best of prevailing market conditions. One of the benefits of swing trading over day trading is that you will mostly be saving your trading capital through buying and holding for a couple of days.

However, there are some challenges related to stocks for days or weeks at a time. One of these challenges includes events and news that occur overnight. Nevertheless, even with these risks, you are still able to find a suitable stock to trade.

There are three basic approaches used to determine the most appropriate stock depending on your preferred trading style. These are technical analysis, major events or catalysts, and fundamental analysis. You can choose your preferred style to begin your hunt for the most ideal stock.

The Initial Steps

The first thing you need to do is find out if there are any major events expected to happen. These are events that will have a direct impact on stock prices, for example, earnings reports. It is important to do this because not only are these events predictable but provide an excellent chance for any serious swing trader.

There are a couple of places to check for events. The internet is one such place. Search the internet for upcoming events in the world of finance, and sometimes, even politics. Political announcements can affect business in a huge way.

You will also need to use technical analysis. This is essential if you are to find some potential trades. Technical analysis also comes in handy when there is a known catalyst that can enable a bullish price movement. It provides the necessary information needed to identify suitable trades. It also helps when there is a catalyst that encourages a bullish pattern.

Technical Analysis

This is the best and most popular approach to find trades that are used by most swing traders. Your trading platform should have a screener that you can use. If it does not come with one, then you can use a free one such as Finviz. Start by examining technical patterns on a regular basis and preferably at night in order to note the ones that are just about to break out or rebound.

You can also search for stocks that experienced a large upward movement in price direction followed by a brief pullback. In fact, this is what swing traders do most of the time. They try to identify a stock that has had a major rally followed by a pullback.

Spend some time filtering through different stocks and identify a couple that you can swing trade. Once this is done, you will then have to come up with a trading plan. A good trading plan implies that you have determined an appropriate entry point, the most suitable stop-loss point, and the best point to collect profits. It is crucial to consolidate your gains at some point, even if the stock continues to gain at price. Should this be the case, then you should consolidate your profits and get back in with a new plan.

Having a good trading plan is crucial for your success. Trading without one is akin to setting yourself up for failure. Therefore, come up with a plan and a reliable risk management strategy. Risk management helps you manage the exposure of your trading capital so that you limit your losses. Without a proper one, you could lose most of your trading capital and put a strain on your trading.

Executing a Trade

Now that you have identified stock to trade and come up with a trading plan, the next step should be to execute the trade. As soon as you do, you will have to keep yourself updated with the latest happening in the world of finance and perhaps even politics. Watch out for any upcoming events and then weight their strengths in terms of affecting your stock's price movement.

Also, be on the lookout for volatility as this is your friend. A prolonged uptrend is never a good thing. When the stock has an uptrend, you should hope to see a reversal in direction for a brief period before the uptrend resumes. This countertrend provides excellent entry points. It also provides information on potential profit-take points as we as points to exit trades or stop-loss points.

You will eventually have to exit your trades. Hopefully, these will have earned you some attractive profits in a short period. After exiting your trades, you need to take a pen and a notebook then note down all the things that took place. Write down what steps you took, what worked for you, and possibly what did not work. Put down the reasons that affected your trades and if they were profitable or not.

If you do not write down details of the trade explaining what worked and what did not, then you are very likely to repeat any mistakes in your next trade. Any lessons learned need to be entered into a journal. This way, you will note all the positives as well as any negatives so as to improve future trades.

The best aspect of swing trading is that you require less energy and less time to trade compared to day trading. It strikes a nice balance between long-term trading and day trading. If you are concerned about holding overnight positions, then you need to know that swing trading is one of the most popular and most profitable forms of generating income and profitability.

Chapter 4 - Long vs. Short

The price of a stock will either go down, go up, or move sideways. When you enter into the market as a swing trader, you are expecting that the stock is going to either go up or it will go down. If you think that the stock will see an increase in its price, then you must purchase it. This move is going to be considered "going long" or having a "long position" in that stock. For example, if you are long 100 shares of Facebook Inc., it means that you purchased 100 shares of this company and you are making the prediction that you will be able to sell them at a higher price later on and earn a nice profit.

That one is pretty easy to understand, but what if you are looking at a stock and you expect that the price is going to decrease? When this situation occurs, you can choose to borrow shares and then later sell them with the expectation that you will purchase them back at a lower price and make a profit later on. At this point, you may be wondering how it is possible for you to sell shares that you do not own or that you do not hold in your account?

This is pretty simple. Brokerages have a mechanism that will allow a trader to borrow the shares. When you end up selling shares you do not actually own, it means you are "going short" or "being short" on a stock. When a trader says that they are short on a stock, it means they borrowed shares from the broker and then sold them with the expectations that the price will drop, and they will be able to replace those shares by purchasing them later at a lower price.

When you are setting up an account to trade, you will probably need to take the time to fill out some additional forms with the broker so that you can take this short position with a stock. You should also have an idea that this option can be riskier compared to just going long or purchasing a stock, so you must be active there to manage the position.

Short selling can be an important tool for you as a swing trader because the prices of the stocks are usually going to drop much faster than they will go up. It is a good rule of thumb to say that stocks are going to fall three times faster than they rise. This is often because of the human psyche; the fear of loss is more powerful than the desire for a gain.

When the stock starts to move down, shareholders are going to fear that they will have to lose their profits or gains, and they move to sell that quickly. This selling activity is going to feed into more selling as shareholders continue to take the profits and traders start to shorten. This additional shorting activity adds to the downward pressure that is there on the price. This sends the price of the stock into a strong decline, which means that short sellers are able to make a good amount of profits while long traders and other investors are going to enter panic mode and may try to dump their shares to protect themselves.

Knowing this information can make it easier to do the trades that you want. It can help you to figure out which position you would like to enter based on how the market or that particular stock is doing at the time. This also shows you that it is possible to get into the market and make profits, no matter which direction you think the market is heading.

Chapter 5 - The Art of Selling Short

One of the biggest pieces of advice you will hear from other traders is that you have to buy low and sell high if you want to make the best profit. This makes complete sense. Think about how retail markets work. Stores will often buy their stock at a lower price than what they sell them for. For example, the store owners might be able to purchase a notebook for $1.00 apiece, but when they put the notebook out on their shelves, they will most likely raise the price, which means you could be buying the notebooks for $1.50, which gives the store a 0.50 cent profit on each notebook they sell.

You want to think the same when you are trading stocks. You need to make sure that when you complete your trading plan for that particular stock that you set a stop-loss price as this will tell you how low you are willing to go. For example, if you decide you do not want less than a dollar loss on a stock, you will set your stop-loss price at a dollar less than you paid for the stock. Of course, you hope you will make a profit, which means that you will sell the stock at a higher price than what you paid for.

A bull market occurs when the stock market is doing well, and prices are rising. A bear market occurs when the stock market prices are dropping. So, when it comes to a bear market, you might ask why people trade as there is not a way for them to make a profit.

However, there is a way that traders can continue to make a profit when the stock market is seeing low numbers and this is through a technique called short selling.

How Short Selling Works?

Unless you become a day trader, most traders will believe that they will hold on to their stock for a good period. Of course, when it comes to swing trading, you will not—or should not—hold on to a stock for longer than a couple of months. With that stated, there are many beginning traders who feel that they are going to start trading and hold the stock for as long as possible as this will give them their best profit. If this is what you are thinking, you are looking more towards investing than trading.

The basic definition of short selling is when a trader takes on stock knowing that he or she is going to sell it after it has fallen in value. Of course, this is something that you are typically told not to do. However, there are many people who have used this position during bear markets and have found that it can be profitable. But you are probably wondering how, if the price has lowered, the trader makes a profit from short selling. The truth of this trick is simple—the trader never actually takes ownership of the stock. Now your next question might be how a trader can sell a stock and receive a profit when he or she does not even own the stock. To look at this in a more basic way, let us look at it in two parts.

First, you have the part where the trader borrows the stock. This is usually done through a loan, which is similar to borrowing money from the bank. This means that the trader fully intends to buy the stock he sold back, which brings us to the second point. Because the stock prices continue to decline, the trader knows that he or she will be buying back the stock at a lower price than what they sold it for. Once they rebuy the stock, they send it back to the original owner which closes out the loan, and the trader was able to make a bit of profit.

In order to start short selling, you will open a margin account through your broker. This account will use your profits in your account as collateral, just as a car is used as collateral for a vehicle loan. This means that if you are unable to repay your broker back in any way, your broker still receives the money as he or she can take it right out of your account. Furthermore, you need to note that you must be able to follow the 2:1 ratio when it comes to short selling. This means that your account must have at least 50% of what you are asking to borrow. For example, if you are asking to borrow $10,000 then you will have to have $5,000 in your account.

You need to be able to sell the stock to the first willing buyer. There is not a huge time-frame for short selling. In fact, it tends to happen very quickly. Then, once the stock has sold, you have to go to the open market with that money and find a lower price for that stock. As you are doing this, it is important to remember that you have to buy back as many shares as you borrowed. Once you decide on your stocks, you will then inform your broker, who will make the transaction through your margin account. From there, your broker will receive his or her funds and you will receive the remaining profit.

The Risks of Short Selling

Of course, there is a lot of risks when it comes to short selling. The biggest risk is that you can never really tell the future. No matter how much you analyze charts or the general stock market conditions, such as if it is a bull or bear market, you will never be able to officially tell what a stock or the market is going to do. Because of this, one of your biggest risks is that you will have to buy back the stock at a higher price than what you sold it as. If this happens, you will take a loss instead of making the profit.

Another great risk when short selling is that you can get yourself into debt. Think of this—if you are unable to make a profit and you borrowed $20,000, this means you only have about $10,000 in your account. Therefore, not only will your broker take all the money in your account, but you still have to pay back the remaining $10,000.

Short selling is very strategic, which can be risky, especially for a beginner. It can seem like a very strange way to do things during an economic downturn. In fact, many beginners often question if short selling is even legal. Which it is, is completely legal and is known to be a popular practice when the stock market is in bull conditions. However, because of its strategy and its risks, it can also be confusing for a beginner, even though you will be working with your broker.

Therefore, like with any other strategy, you want to make sure that you fully understand everything there is about short selling from the process to its risks before you decide to take on this technique during poor stock market conditions. While short selling occurs in a way that is meant to protect the trader's account, you need to realize that you can still bring yourself into debt if the process does not work as well as it should. You also need to verify that you go through the same trading plan, research and following all your rules and guidelines before you decide to short sell. Understanding exactly what the stock market and the stock is doing will help limit your chance of a huge loss and, potentially, bringing yourself into debt.

Chapter 6 - Bull vs. Bear Market

There are dozens of new trading terms that you will learn along your journey, and two of the most common terms are bull and bear. These terms are two types of markets that focus on the current conditions within the stock market. They will often help you in deciding if you should take on a trade or not.

Bull Market

When the conditions of the market are doing well, it is referred to as a bull market. This means that not only are the stock market trends on the rise, but unemployment is low, and most people tend to not struggle as much financially. For a trader, bull markets can make it easier to pick stocks because the majority of the stocks are doing well.

Even though the conditions are great when it comes to the bull market, it does not mean that there are no dangers associated with this type of market. One of the biggest problems with bull markets is known as a bubble. What happens is things seem to be going so well with trading that many traders will over evaluate the positive conditions. Basically, the stock market prices get too high. This can cause the conditions to not follow in their traditional manner and soon the good conditions will burst.

Bear Market

The bear market is the exact opposite of the bull market. In a bear market, the conditions are not great as unemployment will be high and the stock market trends will be on a downward spiral. The biggest problem for traders when it comes to a bear market is that it is riskier for them to take on stocks. Of course, this does not mean that they stop trading. Instead, they just become more cautious of the stocks they pick and do their best to find ones that will turn a decent profit.

Some traders during this time might stick to blue-chip stocks. These are stocks that are shared from the most powerful companies you can think of today, such as Target, Walmart, Apple, Amazon, and Microsoft. However, if these are not your targeted stocks or you are not comfortable taking on these types of stocks, it is best to remain in your comfort zone, especially during bear market conditions.

When faced with the bear market, most traders will do something called short selling. This is when they hold a stock for the shortest time possible as it will give them a more decent profit, or at least they will not lose as much money. With short selling, traders do not actually buy the stocks. Instead, they borrow the stocks and then sell them. Unfortunately, this can be a very risky business for beginners. Furthermore, short selling carries its own set of risks.

One of the biggest reasons why short selling is not meant for beginners is because it can become very tricky. In reality, you are often gambling with your money as you work towards trying to make a profit through borrowing and selling. There are very specific times that you need to find in order to short sell and make the best profit. Of course, any trader is able to accomplish short selling and become profitable. Like with any other factor in trading, you will just need to make sure that you do your research, speak with your advisor, and understand the process.

Chapter 7 - Account, Tools and Platforms

Normally, foreign exchange involves selling and purchasing of different currencies across the world. The number of participants in this market is very large therefore the liquidity is very high. The most unique aspect of the forex trade is that individual traders can compete against large institutions such as hedge funds and commercial banks; all one needs to do is to select the right account and set it up.

There are different types of accounts, but the traders have three main options, namely mini accounts, standard accounts, and managed accounts. Each account has its own advantages and disadvantages. The type of account that one opts for depends on factors such as the size of initial capital, risk tolerance levels, and the hours one has to analyze the charts either daily or at different intervals.

Mini Trading Accounts

Simply put, a mini account is one that allows the trader to transact using mini lots. For most brokerage firms, one mini lot equals to 10,000 units. That is equal to 1/10 of a standard account. Brokerage firms offer mini lots to attract new traders who are still hesitant to trade with bigger accounts or those who do not have the investment funds required.

The advantages of mini accounts include low risk, low capital required, and flexibility. The trader can trade in increments of 10,000 units therefore if he or she is inexperienced, does not have to worry about blowing through their account and capital. Experienced traders can use this method to test new strategies without excessive risk. A mini account can be opened with as little as $100, $250 or $500 and the leverage can go up to 400:1. A risk management plan is the key to successful trading; and in the case of selecting lots, a trader can minimize the risk by buying a number of mini lots. Remember that one standard lot is equal to about 10 mini lots and diversification reduces risk.

The main disadvantage of mini accounts is a low reward. Lower risk translates to a lower reward. A mini lot account can only produce $1 per pip movement if it is trading 10,000 lots. In a standard account, one pip movement equals to $10.

A subset of the mini account is the micro account which is offered by some online brokers. This account has very little risk and also very little reward. The trade is 1,000 base currency units and one pip movement earns or losses 10 cents. These accounts are best suited for traders who have very little knowledge about forex trade and one can open using as little as 25 dollars.

Standard Trading Accounts

The standard trading accounts are the most common for traders, especially the experienced ones. These accounts give trader access to lots of currency worth 100,000 units each. This, however, does not mean that a trader has to put $100,000 in the account as capital so as to trade. The rules of leverage and margin mean that all a trader need is $1,000 to have a margin account.

The main advantage of this account is the large reward that one might reap with the right strategy and predictions. One pip movement earns $10. Again, individuals who own such accounts get better services and perks because of the upfront capital invested in the account.

The disadvantages include high initial capital and potential for loss. The kind of capital required to set up a standard account can deter many traders from venturing into it. Again, the higher the risk, the higher the returns and the vice versa holds. A standard account trader has a higher risk of loss because if a lot of falls with 100 pips, he or she losses $1,000. Such losses can be devastating for beginner traders.

Managed Trading Accounts

Managed accounts are accounts where one puts in the capital but does not make the decisions to sell or buy. Such accounts are handled by account managers such as stockbrokers and stock managers. In this case, the traders set objectives for the managers (the expected returns, risk management) and they have to meet them.

Managed accounts are categorized into two major types, namely Pooled funds and Individual accounts. In pooled funds, the money of different investors is put into an investment vehicle referred to as a mutual fund, and the profits generated are shared. The accounts are further classified by risk tolerance. If a trader is looking for higher returns, he or she may put the money in a high-risk/reward account while those looking for long-term steady income can invest in lower-risk accounts. Under managed accounts, the individual accounts are managed by a broker each in its own capacity, unlike the pooled funds where the manager uses all the money together.

The main advantage of managed accounts is that one gets professional advice and guidance. An experienced professional forex account manager will be making the decisions and this is a benefit that one can use. Again, a trader gets to trade without having to spend hours analyzing the charts and watching for developments.

One disadvantage that deters traders from venturing into this account is the high price. One should be aware that the majority of managed accounts require one to put in at least $2,000 in the pooled account and $10,000 for the individual accounts. To add to this cost, the managers are entitled to a commission which is calculated monthly or yearly. The managed accounts are also very inflexible for the trader. If he or she sees an opportunity to trade, he or she will not be able to make a move but will rely on the manager to decide.

Note

It is advisable for a swing trader to use the demo accounts offered by brokers before investing in real money, regardless of the account he or she opts to use. Demo accounts allow one to practice without risk and also to try out different strategies. One rule that every trader should apply is to never invest in a real account unless they are completely satisfied with it. One of the main differences between success and failure in forex exchange is the account selected.

Opening an Account

Forex exchange has been around for very many years and some say that it is as old as the invention of national currencies. Over the years, the market has grown so much so that it is the biggest market across the world. However, it has not been accessible to the public as easily as it is today. From the 1990s, when the era of the internet begun, many retail Forex brokers have established routes through which anyone can trade in currencies so long as they can access the internet and have some money. There is a lot of hype and information about forex trade on the internet, but not everybody understands how to select and open an account.

Currently, opening a forex account has become as easy as opening a bank account or another type of brokerage account. Some of the typical requirements are a name, phone number, address, email, a password, account currency type, country of citizenship, date of birth, employment status, and tax ID or social security number. Opening an account may also require one to answer some financial questions such as their net worth, annual income, trading objectives, and trading experience. Before one starts to trade on the foreign exchange market, they should make some considerations to ensure that they have a positive, secure, and successful experience.

The Right Broker

The first step to trading well is to find the right broker. The activities of forex exchange are decentralized and there are hardly any regulations. Because of the over-the-counter nature, traders are advised to identify a reliable broker. This involves conducting researches on the reputation of the broker to identify if there is a history of irregular practices. One may also want to comprehensively understand the services offered by the particular broker before setting up an account. While some brokerages support basic and plain vanilla activities, others offer very sophisticated trading platforms. Some brokers will offer the trader analytical resources to support better decision making while others will not.

Again, a trader should assess the fees and commissions for different brokers. The majority of brokers charge some fees for their services through the bid-ask spread and, in many cases, it is not a large percentage. However, some brokerages have some other fees and commissions and they might be hidden from the trader. When one is considering the extra costs, he or she should check if it is worthwhile.

The Procedure

Opening a foreign exchange account is not hard, but traders should have a few things to get started. The trader will have to provide some identifying information such as name, phone number, country of origin, et cetera. Besides, the trader will be required to state his or her trade intentions and their level of knowledge and experience in the trade. The steps of opening an account may vary depending on the brokerage firm, but normally it involves:

- Accessing the website of the broker and study the accounts available. The accounts include small ones where the trader can trade with minimum capital such as mini accounts or the sophisticated accounts designed for experienced traders such as standard trading account.
- Completing an application form.

- Getting registered (user name and password) to access the account.
- Log in to the client portal and arrange for a transfer of money from the bank to the forex account. These deposits can be done through credit or debit cards, checks, or electronic transfers.
- Once the funds are transferred, the trader is ready to start trading. But before that, he or she may study the recommendations made by the brokers or extra services offered such as simulator programs.

Online Trading

It refers to buying and selling stocks or other assets by the use of a broker's internet-based website or trading platform. Currencies, futures, options, ETFs, mutual funds, bonds, and stocks can all be traded online. It is called self-directed investing or e-trading.

As mentioned above, in a split of a second you can trade stocks and other financial instruments such as the Dollar or Euro, some commodities such as Gold or Oil as well as main market indices.

One more advantage of online trading is that the improvement in the rate of which trades can be implemented and settled, since there is no demand for paper-based files to be reproduced, registered and entered into a digital format. Once an investor opens a buy position on the internet, the trade is set in a database that assesses for the very best price by searching all the marketplace trades that trade the inventory in the investor's currency. The market with the very best price fits the buyer with a vendor and sends the confirmation to the purchaser's agent and the seller's agent. All this process can be achieved within minutes of opening a trade, in comparison to making a telephone call that requires several confirmation steps before the representative can input the purchase.

Chapter 8 - Options and Forex Swing Trading

Options and forex swing trading are two types of trading strategies that are often overlooked. Options are when you create an agreement. Through this agreement, the options buyer has the right to buy and sell once the stock hits a certain price. It doesn't matter when this happens, as soon as the stock gets to the set price, the steps are taken to complete the agreement. Forex is often overlooked because it focuses on currencies. This means that you have to have pairs in order to make a trade. For example, you would pair the American dollar with the Canadian dollar.

Options Swing Trading

When you use options trading as your strategy, you are using the options market. The types of financial instruments, typically called options, which are used in this market are ETFs and bonds. Options are not run on the stock market because they are not considered stocks. While there is still a risk involved, it does decrease because you are able to stop the agreement you set at any time. There is nothing in the options market that states you need to follow through with the agreement.

There are two main types of options:

- A Call option is an agreement allowing you to buy shares at a later time and date. This information is often written into the agreement.
- A Put option is an agreement allowing you to sell shares at a later time and date. Like the call option, this information is typically included in the agreement.

Many times, the agreed-upon time and date are known as the expiration date. This means that from the moment of the agreement to the expiration time, a trader can decide to buy or sell the specified option.

Like with other types of markets, there is different language associated with options trading. While you can use many of the same types of strategies as swing trading, you will want to ensure you understand the language.

You know you will enjoy options trading if you are interested in statistics and calculations as options trading is completely about calculated risk. With this in mind, there are two types of volatility you have to be aware of:

1. **Implied volatility** is when you are looking at what the market stated the volatility will look like in the future. This is what you base your decision on when making an agreement.

2. **Historical volatility** is when you look at the price fluctuations of your financial instrument throughout a whole year. This means you will look month-to-month, week-to-week, and day-to-day.

Forex Swing Trading

Before you get into forex swing trading, you want to take time to study some of the most popular currency pairs, such as the Euro and American dollar (EUR/USD) and the American dollar and Canadian dollar (USD/CAD). What this means is you will sell one pair while you are buying another. It's similar to how you convert your country's money to a different country's currency when on vacation.

When it comes to forex pairs, there are four categories you need to be aware of.

Minor pairs are traded, but not often. Most of these pairs do not include the American dollar. For example, they might include Japan and China's currency against each other.

Major pairs are the currencies that are traded often. These pairs typically include the American dollar and make up around 80% of all forex trades.

Regional pairs are strictly classified by regions.

Exotics pair a smaller currency against a major currency.

Along with these categories, there are three types of forex markets:

- Forward forex market is an agreement to buy or sell currency at a specific price. This agreement typically includes the date or a range of dates that this trade can take place.
- Spot forex market is when you make the trade on the spot. This is one of the most common forex markets.
- Futures forex market is similar to the forex market but it's an exchange-traded contract. This market focuses on a certain date and price for an exchange.

One of the nice parts about forex swing trading is you don't have to have a certain amount of money. There are a few strategies that will work with less than $1,000. Of course, you can use the same guidelines as you would with larger amounts of money. For example, you can put only 1% into your trade.

Because forex is a different market, there are different basics you need to know. For example, there are pips in the forex market. The pip's value depends on the size of the trade.

Forex is a bit different from the stock market because it is run on a global scale. This means it is typically open, at least Monday through Friday. Instead of remaining open from around 9:30 A.M. to 4:00 P.M., the forex market opens on Monday morning and then closes on Friday afternoon. This means it is open 24 hours a day throughout the week.

This doesn't mean that you need to pay attention to the market 24 hours a day, 5 days a week if you want to be a forex trader. But it does mean that you can choose to trade overnight, during the day, or mix it up. For example, you can follow the typical day schedule like a stock swing trader would do or you can start trading at 5:00 P.M. and stop trading around 11:00 P.M. Even though the forex market is open overnight doesn't mean there isn't an overnight risk. The risk comes with your schedule. What this means is whenever you have financial instruments, such as currencies or stocks, in your portfolio and you are not watching the market, you are running a risk. Of course, this doesn't mean you always need to keep your eye on the market. But you also don't want to allow your trades to sit for a long period of time without ensuring your companies are still doing well.

Chapter 9 - Risk Management for Swing Trading

Discipline is one of the hardest things to ace. In the meantime, it is the most significant component of effective exchanging. It is dependent upon each merchant to set up a pre-showcase routine and construct solid exchanging propensities.

You ought to endeavor to accomplish discipline on the off chance that you ever would like to accomplish any degree of exchanging achievement. Exchanging control is polished most of the time, in each exchange, every single day.

Along these lines, to give you a hand, this blog entry goes for uncovering the 10 brilliant guidelines of exchanging discipline. You should consistently condition yourself to be restrained. On the off chance that you need to be a genuine broker, then read through the standards consistently before the exchanging session starts. It shouldn't take over three minutes to peruse them. Think about the activity as reminding you how to behave all through the exchanging session.

1. Adhere to a Proven Trading Method

Furthermore, do not transform it. In the event that you have a demonstrated technique however it does not appear to work in a given exchanging session, do not return home that night and attempt to devise another. In the event that your strategy works for more than one-portion of the exchanging sessions, at that point stay with it. Keep in mind, the Holy Grail of exchanging is cash the executives.

2. Effectively Trade the First Three Hours of Each Major Session

It is basic information that the Forex market exchanges 24 hours every day. In any case, not those hours are practical for day exchanging. In the event that you are an informal investor, you need to focus on the accompanying exchanging perspectives: unpredictability, force, bearing, pattern and difference.

Also, you have to settle on positional exchanging and scalping. Take positions that appear to be the most self-evident, on the grounds that these are the most ideal approach to amplify your benefits. You can figure out how to recognize easy decision arrangements utilizing our investigation and online courses.

Additionally, focus on your exchanging plan. The initial three hours of each significant session are typically the best as far as force, pattern, and retracement. It is then that we broker will in general locate the best exchanging potential outcomes.

3. The Market Rewards You for Your Discipline

Exchanging with control should (all being great) compensate you with a positive cash stream. The purpose of exchanging with control is to have more pips in your record and less pips out. The one consistent truth concerning the business sectors is that exchanging with control ought to furnish you with greater benefit potential.

4. Consistency is Confidence

How great does it feel to have the option to turn on your exchanging stage the morning realizing that, on the off chance that you play by the guidelines, the likelihood of fruitful exchanging day is generally high? The appropriate response? Great! Keep in mind: If you make somewhat consistently, at that point you have earned the privilege to exchange greater.

5. Try not to Let a Winner Become a Loser

We have all abused this standard every once in a while. Be that as it may, it ought to be our objective to invest more energy not to abuse it later on. What I am talking about here is the voracity factor. The market has compensated you by moving toward your position. Be that as it may, you are not happy with a little victor. Along these lines, you clutch the exchange, the desire for a bigger increase, just to watch the market turn and move against you. Obviously, unavoidably you presently falter and the exchange further weakens into a misfortune, now and then considerably.

The brilliant standard I use is–benefit taking. When we exchange on an intraday premise, we have to utilize benefit stops. When we are in benefit, we have to move our Stop-Loss into a benefit in this manner, verifying benefits. That way we ought to ensure our benefits. To perceive how this is done for all intents and purposes, I propose you visit my live exchanging online courses.

6. Try not to Chase the Markets

Actually, you ought to abstain from bouncing on a cargo train. This may suck you into a winding of fate as you understand the business sectors may betray you. Quietly sit tight for the arrangement. The business sectors resemble a shadow. On the off chance that you pursue it, you'll never get it. In the event that you stop, it will grasp you.

Proficient merchants that pick Admiral Markets will be satisfied to realize that they can exchange totally chance free with a FREE demo exchanging account. Rather than going to the live markets and putting your capital in danger, you can dodge the hazard out and out and essentially practice until you are prepared to change to live exchanging.

7. Remember EOD–End of Day Trading

At the point when the London session is going to end, regardless you have roughly a few extra hours to adventure advertised developments. In the event that you neglect to utilize this time, your exchanging may stop in its tracks until the Tokyo session opens. EOD exchanging is extraordinary, as you more often than not have to exchange against the pattern. Why?

Since when most day exchanging market movers take benefits, the cost follows. Each end of a purchase position is a programmed sell again into the market. The enormous bit of leeway of EOD exchanging is that it doesn't require consistent observing which, thus, makes it perfect for dealers with a normal everyday employment.

8. You Are a Long-Distance Runner

Have you at any point wanted to exchange while not having the option to do as such in light of the fact that the value in your record is excessively low and your specialist probably will not enable you to exchange except if you submit more assets? That occurs on the off chance that you go out on a limb. Huge misfortunes hurt, and they hurt excessively. Use influence keenly. Try not to hazard over 4% per exchange. Keep in mind, you need to have the option to exchange one more day.

9. Pursue Your Trading Routine

Your exchanging routine should comprise a significant market hours trading, pre-advertise investigation and end of day (EOD) hours.

Never attempt to break your exchanging schedule. Pursue real markets and exchange just during the significant markets. These include: New York, London and Tokyo markets.

The value moves all the more detectably during significant market sessions, so you can disregard minor markets. Significant markets furnish you with an incredible number of arrangements as well.

Truth be told, you can as of now check the day's monetary schedule for any solid financial reports that may impact your arrangements; at that point move to value activity investigation, to check whether the costs have gotten through significant help or opposition levels. My recommendation is to exchange drifting markets.

10. It is a Step-by-Step Process

Attempt to utilize exacerbating. Aggravating is an incredible method to add benefits to your benefits. It is entirely appropriate for smaller estimated accounts. At last, you may even have the option to assemble a six-make sense of whole of two-figure account.

By following these 10 brilliant principles of exchanging discipline, those gainful days may before long become increasingly visit. This is because you will have adopted perfect, risk-averse techniques for swing trading.

Chapter 10 - Technical Issues

Technical examination endeavors to conjecture future value developments by analyzing past organic market changes as that are reflected in changes in costs after some time. Most traders utilize technical investigation to get a "major picture" on a venture's value history. Indeed, even essential traders will look at a graph to check whether they're purchasing at a reasonable value, selling at a patterned top, or entering a rough, sideways market.

Technical Analysts Make a Few Key Assumptions

All data about market essentials are reflected in value information. States of mind, contrasting assessments, and other market basics need not be considered. They are altogether reflected in the cost at a given minute. The value changes as new data end up accessible.

History rehashes itself in ordinary, genuinely unsurprising patterns. These patterns, created by value developments, are called signals. A technical examiner will probably reveal a present market's sign by inspecting past market signals.

Costs move in patterns. Technical investigators accept value variances are not arbitrary and erratic. When an up, down, or sideways pattern has been set up, it, for the most part, will proceed for a period.

Discover Potential Trade Entry and Exit Points

Traders depend on value charts, volume charts, and other scientific portrayals of market information (called thinks about) to attempt to foresee the perfect passage and leave focuses for a trade. A few investigations help distinguish a pattern, while others help decide the quality and manageability of that pattern after some time.

The technical examination can include discipline and limit feeling in your trading plan. It very well may be difficult to screen out key impressions and stick with your entrance and leave focuses as arranged. While no framework is immaculate, technical investigation causes you to see your trading plan through more equitably and impartially.

Value Chart Types

1. **Bar charts**

The most widely recognized sort of outline demonstrating value activity. Each bar speaks to a timeframe–a "period" as short as 1 moment or up to quite a long while. After some time, the bar charts show unmistakable value patterns.

2. **Candle charts**

Rather than a simple bar, every candle shows the high, low, opening and shutting cost for that timeframe it speaks to. Candle patterns give more noteworthy visual detail as they create.

Point and figure charts

Point and figure patterns look like bar graph patterns, aside from Xs and Os are utilized to check alters in value course. Point and figure charts utilize a time scale to connect a specific day with a specific value activity.

Technical Indicator Types

1. **Trend**

Trend indicators smooth value information out, with the goal that a persevering up, down, or sideways pattern can be effectively observed. (Models: moving averages, pattern lines).

2. **Strength**

Strength indicators portray the force of market assessment on a specific cost by analyzing the market positions taken by different market members. Volume or open intrigue are the fundamental elements of solidarity indicators.

3. Volatility

"Volatility" alludes to the greatness of day-to-day value variances, whatever their directional pattern. Changes in unpredictability will, in general, envision changes in costs. (Model: Bollinger Bands).

4. Cycle

Cycle indicators show rehashing market patterns from repetitive occasions, for example, seasons or decisions. Cycle indicators decide the planning of a specific market pattern. (Model: Elliott Wave).

5. Support/resistance

Support and resistance depict the value levels where markets over and again rise or fall and afterward turn around. This wonder is ascribed to fundamental market interest. (Model: Trend Lines).

6. Momentum

Momentum indicators decide the quality or shortcomings of a pattern as it advances after some time. Energy is most elevated when a pattern begins and least when the pattern changes. New data makes vulnerability, which will show a pattern and may switch it.

At the point when cost and energy veer, it proposes shortcoming. On the off chance that value boundaries happen with powerless force, it flags a finish of development toward that path. On the off chance that energy is drifting unequivocally and costs are level, it flags a potential alter in value course.

Conclusion

I wish everyone a complete success on their journey to make this happen. But we have to be honest and admit that getting there is not necessarily going to be easy. There are going to be mistakes along the way. You may even lose a significant amount of money. One of the traits that a successful trader has to have is you have to be persistent. That includes having the ability of two being able to bounce back from defeats. The main thing when it comes to running into trouble swing trading is that you need to learn from your mistakes. Hopefully, readers will not get involved in trading, have one or two bad trades, and give up. If you get in that situation, go back, study the fundamentals of swing trading, and look at the mistakes you made the call sure trades to go bad. Then dust yourself off and get up and try again.

In the end, though, swing trading may not be for everyone. So do not get depressed if it does not work out for you. Along the way, however, something to consider is applying swing trading in different markets if you find that your first stab at it does not work. One thing that I know was going to happen is a lot of people are going to be interested in swing trading on Forex. For some reason, the currency exchange market holds a lot of appeal for a lot of people. And that is fine as far as it goes. Many people are actually pretty successful on the market. At the same time a lot of people or not, because that is a really touchy market. So, my advice if you decide to start off trading Forex, and it does not work out for you, is that you should not give up on swing trading altogether. Instead, try regrouping and then, even though it is not quite as exciting, try swing-trading stocks instead.

The same problem might arise when it comes to trading options. I have a lot of experience trading options. While I have had a lot of fun doing it, you need to be aware if you have not tried it yet, that trading options can be very tricky. It is also something that gives you the opportunity on a bad day to watch your money melt away. Options are very sensitive to price changes in the underlying stock. This can range from a 50% to 100% proportional change. So, what this means is that if the stock rises or falls by a dollar, the price of your option could rise or fall anywhere from $50-$100. An expensive stock says over $200, is not going to be a stock that is undergoing a significant change from a dollar drop in the price. So, you can see that options can be a security that magnifies both gains and losses. The upshot of this is that options trading is not for the thin-skinned. Something else to consider is that options are actually a little bit complicated. Some new traders who may be intrigued by the idea might not really understand what they are doing and they might get themselves into trouble as a result.

Note that if you start off trading options, and you find that it is not working out, that is not necessarily a reason to give up swing trading. Again, what I would recommend it if you follow this path and that happen is you should consider dropping options but continuing swing trading would something simple like stocks.

People might be put off by the higher price of stocks, but you can start off small and working way up with time. Do not start off thinking about trading 50 or 100 shares at a time. To learn the ropes, you can even start off only trading a single share if that is all you can afford. Even though that is not something that is going to make you any significant money, it would serve as a great training ground, and you would learn how to enter and that your position at the right times. It would also provide a way for you to learn how to do your technical analysis on the real data without really having much risk on the line. Then, as time goes on, you can increase the number of shares that you are trading until you get to the point where you are making real money.

Another thing to say is that you should not jump off a cliff. And what I mean by this, is that you should not quit your job or take other radical actions right away in order to swing trade. In the beginning, at least when you are a swing trading stocks or Forex, you can certainly do it on a part-time basis. It is not necessary to sit at the computer all day long the way that a day trader has to do.

www.ingramcontent.com/pod-product-compliance
Lightning Source LLC
LaVergne TN
LVHW021133031125
824896LV00010B/798